Wh

Why Flags

Why Flags

Why Flags

Why Flags

Linda K. Donnelly

Why Flags

Why Flags

Resource Ordering and Information:

Linda Donnelly
Behold His Presence
Telephone: (717) 609-2623
Email: beholdhis@hotmail.com
Facebook: Behold His Presence ~ custom designed Dance, Worship Flags and Banners ~

Dedication

I dedicate my book "Why Flags" to my Lord Jesus Christ, who has been with me guiding me through this whole process of writing. I am thankful for Your faithfulness to me, Lord. I depend on You, Lord, for guidance and wisdom every day. I do not take Your Word for granted because it is life and truth. It has truly changed my life, and I will be eternally grateful to You. "Your word is a lamp to my feet and a light to my path." Psa. 119:105

*I would be remiss if I did not give honor and gratitude to my spiritual father and mother, **Pastors Philip and Gwen Thornton**, who have been supportive in teaching the Word of God, praying for me, giving me guidance and counsel, and going the extra mile. I have been under your teaching for 18 years now and am very appreciative for that. Being trained up under your anointing has matured me into the woman God has created and called me to be. Your close walk with God and your godly example has encouraged me throughout the years. Your strong and militant stand for godly principles makes me strong. Therefore, I have much respect and love for you.*

*I am thankful for my brother in Christ and friend, **Calvin Rattray**, who I met at a conference. Calvin, you are one of the happiest persons I know. You fill my life with testimonies and expand my thinking with new truths from God. You always encourage me when I need a lift. Your LOVE for God is amazing, and so is how you express His love to me. Your creativity inspires me with your harmonica ministry and Hosanna Maranatha Ministries, especially your dance and how you use my flags and finger ribbons to worship the Lord. Thank you so much for encouraging me to write this book and also for your business ideas you have shared with me. God surely has BLESSED me with your friendship. Thank you for being you!*

Why Flags

I am thankful for my friend, business buddy, and editor, **Cheryl Hawkins**. I will never forget the good times we have had over the years. First and foremost, thank you for the many years we spent on designing my seminar and conference information and training materials; and secondly, for helping me with this book – and yes, laughing and crying. We make a great team. I want you to know you will always have a special place in my heart. You have always been there for me through thick and thin. THANK YOU FROM THE BOTTOM OF MY HEART. You are a precious friend. Through the years of our friendship, we have done nothing but to strengthen each other. I AM TRULY BLESSED TO CALL YOU MY FRIEND. I love you, my friend. ". . . I thank my God through Jesus Christ for you. . ." (Romans 1:8a).

A ram in the thicket – yes, that is what **Mary Eisenacher** has been for me. Yes, Mary answered the call to help me to complete the book draft that I had already started. A friend invited me to Mary's Bible study. When I found out she is an author, I asked her to view a YouTube training on publishing books. She agreed to watch it with me. I knew nothing about publishing books. I had told her that I was looking for someone to help me get my book published. Praise God! She agreed to help me. I was seeking the Lord in December 2018 about getting my book finished, and I heard these words "divine alignment." Mary is part of my divine alignment. I thank God for Mary to take this challenging responsibility to help me complete my book. Thank You, Jesus.

Mary has written many books herself, so I had confidence in her. She also has a ministry that is called Call of the Wild Ministries, Inc. She is a songwriter, worship leader, pulpit minister, and conference host. Mary is spirit-led in everything she does and is on fire for the Lord. She walks in compassion, love, and is kind. I love her smile! Patience is a virtue. Because I am a work in progress with limited electronic experience, she has needed patience with me. (www.CallBytheWildMin.org) From Ruth 1:8b

Why Flags

– *"The Lord deal kindly with you, as you have dealt . . . with me." You see, what you make happen for others, God will make happen for you.*

*Thank you, **Elaine Bish**, White Deer Photography, for providing the cover pictures and the picture on page 12 (Vision and Mission Statement). I appreciate your time and seeding into my ministry. We had a great time at the photo sessions. (www.elainebish.zenfolio.com)*

*I do not want to leave out the ones who were there for me through this experience and who reminded me of the scripture, Ephesians 4:16 that says, "from him the whole body joined and held together by every supporting ligament, grows and builds itself up in love as each part does its work." Thank you, **Lisa Adams**, **Regina Gidcumb**, **Gladys Ogwal**, **Sharon Simmons**, and **Nancy Thompson**.*

Linda K. Donnelly, Author

Acknowledgments

I met Linda at a conference where she taught on the ministry of flags. Since that time, we have communicated with each other. I have purchased from her several flags and finger ribbons for use in the harmonica ministry the Lord has given me, especially for children. Personally, I have used them during devotional time, to which I have been blessed and continue to be blessed. Soon I will be using them in the ministry I have been responsible for - HOSANNA MARANATHA MINISTRIES.

Best wishes to Linda Donnelly and above all, God's blessings. Also, blessings to all who may use these flags and ribbons for God's glory.

Calvin B. Rattray, Operating Minister,
President of Hosanna Maranatha Ministries
Musician, Singer, Harmonica Instructor

Author of:
Rose of Sharon
Royal Kingdom Children
Royal Kingdom Children #2: Brainstorming
Royal Kingdom Sound Encyclopedia Journal
Merry Christmas-Happy New Year 365 Days Journal

Why Flags

Linda is a brilliant, creative, exciting, and talented person to know. She puts love in creating her flags and banners. You can feel the joy, and then the anointing comes forth in praise and worship. Thank you for sharing your God-given talent with others.

Joyce Vanderhorst-Gamble

Linda, my sister in Christ and friend:

CONGRATULATIONS!! After five years of birth pangs, you have a completed work that expresses your passion, your desire, and love for the Lord. I feel as if I was the midwife in your delivery room. When you first asked me to help get your concept or dreams on paper, my first thought was, "How hard can it be to type someone else's ideas?" I loved the fact that most of the witty ideas were downloaded from heaven when we met at our favorite restaurants for our planning sessions; there was something about a delicious salad, soup or grilled cheese sandwich that opened up our minds to create and see Behold His Presence unfold on paper. I have enjoyed working with you, and this publication will be the beginning of more to come as God continues to unlock mysteries and His purpose in you.

Declaring life over you, to you, and for the new places God is going to give you access. Thank you from my heart for the privilege to serve the Lord and worship Him through this assignment. I close with a reminder of the word the Lord gave me for you in 2016.

"Linda, as we were sitting in the presence of God, I could not help but see you were glowing, and the Lord showed me this in the spirit. I saw you being a light in the darkness, that when you are around others, the Light through you, which is the Anointing will push back the darkness and will change the atmosphere from dark to light. The boldness in you

Why Flags

will either bring offense and conviction or deliverance. It will bring you favor where others would not be able to find resources, as you are already experiencing, will be in your path. Do not back up, nor back down, continue to shine!

Later as I was driving home, I also saw fresh oil being applied upon you. Just like an automatic candlewick that burns continually and continuously, when you seem like you are running on empty, or like the wick is getting dimmer, the Lord, the God of more than enough, will provide and give you fresh oil perpetually over and above what you have experienced in the past."

Continue to follow the Lord and be obedient to what He says. The Lord is with you, and His name is in you.

Cheryl Hawkins

Linda came to me for help to do some final editing on this exceptional teaching tool that God has given her. I look forward to hearing about when God takes her to teach and demonstrate this expertise in craftsmanship and delivery for spiritual purposes. This Spring and Summer has been a concentration to help writers. Linda asked for what she needed, and I took on a great deal of time as a copy-ready publisher to help her get through this exhaustive process and turn the work over to another to finish the process of printing. I pulled out all the stops to help her get an excellent composition polished. May it go forth to the nations and all those who need to know what benefit flags can be in praise and worship. Linda is a yielded vessel to God, a student of the Word, and a prayer warrior. She was a joy to collaborate in this work. I believe that God has more spiritual warriors for her to teach and train. Enjoy the reading of this book, and remember that Linda is a custom flag designer who can guide you in your individual or corporate needs.

Why Flags

Mary Eisenacher, Founder & Minister
Call of the Wild Ministries, Inc.
"Helping Others Answer God's Call"

Foreword

I have had the pleasure of reading Linda's book, and in doing so, I found it extremely informative. I had no idea, to be honest with you, just how important and to what degree of worship the colors mean and the movement of flag worship entails [movement in future writing].

I highly recommend this first book of Linda's as your building block to start your journey of flag ministry.

On a more personal note, it has been my experience that when I witness Linda enter into praise and worship with her flag ministry, that I am so inspired by the atmosphere change and by the presence of God that she attracts during her worship. The walls come crashing down, there is a shift in the atmosphere, and healing begins.

Lisa Adams

As a servant and editor in preparing this manuscript for publication, I was not able to grasp ahold of the many variations of flag ministry until asked to make revisions. That is when the referenced scriptures, definitions, and declarations began to come alive. While reflecting upon the process that took place in the birthing of this book through the author, I am convinced that the following scriptures helped to shape her framework and showed her how to express in writing what she felt God had written about her and others called and chosen to carry out His plan through flag ministry.

- "For God has not given us the spirit of fear, but of power and of love, and of a sound mind." 2 Tim. 1:7

Why Flags

- "I can do all things through Christ who strengthens me." Phil. 4:13
- "Let them shout for joy and be glad, who favor my righteous cause; and let them say continually, "Let the LORD be magnified, who has pleasure in the prosperity of His servant." Psa. 35:27
- "Trust in the Lord with all your heart, and lean not on your own understanding; in all your ways acknowledge Him, and He shall direct your paths." Prov. 3:5-6
- "The Lord will open to you His good treasure, the heavens, to give the rain to your land in its season, and to bless all the work of your hand." Deut. 28:12a

It is exciting to see this book be presented to the Earth and watch it change the way one sees how God uses flags and banners. I heard it said that "God downloads movements to us to communicate back to His people. When God has called you to the movement ministry, He will give you the movements." May you be blessed in this reading . . . so that when the hour comes for the Courts of Heaven to call for the flags to be raised on the Earth, there will be a performance in demonstration and power and an understanding that the Lord has commanded a thing.

Cheryl Hawkins

Vision and Mission Statement

Behold His Presence Flag Ministry is a spirit-filled, biblically based presentation, whose primary purpose is to minister to the body of Christ the heart of God through creative expressions of worship, flags, and dance. **Behold His Presence** exists to develop intimacy and closeness with the Father, to equip the people of God through praise, worship, and intercession, and to stir up the gift within. This art of worship instructs the movement of flags, and the meaning of the colors and its biblical context.

Isaiah 59:19b says, "When the enemy comes in like a flood, the Spirit of the Lord will lift up a standard against him." (and put him to flight).

The Author's Testimony

I was born in Mitchell, South Dakota; and during my adolescence, my family and I moved to Pennsylvania. My childhood was difficult in that I was raised in an alcoholic environment. But as far back as I can remember, I loved to go to church. Many of the insecurities I picked up at home were carried into my teens. My outlet was dancing. I would go to every school dance I could. Later, I would learn that the natural and spiritual would many times operate in a parallel fashion and that my love for dancing would one day be translated into my love to worship and dance before King Jesus (as in the natural, so it is in the Spirit).

I got married at a young age and soon after was introduced to Jesus Christ as my Lord and Savior. My new in-laws were believers and were responsible for my new-found faith. Praise God! I then had the awesome privilege of bringing two wonderful children into the world – Wesley and Michelle, and Emma is my granddaughter.

My foundation years in faith were spent in the Assemblies of God denomination, where I became a Sunday School teacher and a coordinator for the Missionettes Girls' Club program. Through many of life's challenges and situations, I have to say God was always by my side. Even in my unfaithfulness, God has been faithful to me. If you can stand the squeeze, God will pull you through.

In the beginning, I made praise tools for my personal use. In 2002, I had a friend that made flags. We chose to make a few and give them away. It was at this junction that I decided to birth the ministry now known as **Behold His Presence***. Using the gift of dance from my father and the gift to sew from my mother . . . the ministry of praise tools, worship accessories, and the flags came to fruition.*

Why Flags

Though it was a slow process, the Lord was faithful in bringing together the details – even the name of the ministry. Little by little, the doors began to open as I continued to express myself through worship, praise, and dance.

While in the presence of God, many times I was delivered from things I could not break through on my own.

I dance with complete abandonment like no one else exists except the Lord.

As far as types of dance . . . it is an inward desire for me to express joy, worship, and warfare. I realize my calling is to lead people into true worship. "But the hour is coming, and now is, when the true worshipers will worship the Father in spirit and truth; for the Father is seeking such to worship Him." John 4:23 Being led to study and do extensive research on all the many facets of the ministry was another component to this task. So within, or under the umbrella of flag ministry, I developed a training packet and study guide that I have used to teach at seminars.

My journey is likened to the birthing of a child. Let us pause and think about what happens during the birth process. There is a seed and conception, there are three trimesters, and then the bundle of joy appears. Next comes the celebration, and then the real journey or responsibility begins. When I knew that the Lord had called me to this responsibility, I felt fulfilled and eager to begin the process. However, the Lord had another plan, I had to go through what felt like abandonment, rejection, dry times, and I questioned whether I was birthing out of season.

There was a huge amount of time invested, financial sacrifice, and lots of tears. At one time, it seemed as if it would not come to fruition. Yes, I even wanted to give up. But God! Jeremiah 29:11 NIV[1] says, "For I know

---

[1] **New International Version** (NIV)

Why Flags

the plans I have for you," declares the LORD, "plans to prosper you and not to harm you, plans to give you hope and a future."

During one of my darkest moments, I heard the Lord say to me, "No man shall close what I have opened to you." I held onto that rhema word. What I also need to share with you is that I had lost my husband during this time. Without the support of him, I found myself reestablishing who I was in Christ and as a person. But even throughout all this time, I never stopped creating, seeing, hearing, building my faith, praying, praising, and worshiping. The Lord said to me during a service, Jeremiah 51:20, "You are my battle ax and weapons of war; and with you will I break in pieces the nations; and with you will I destroy kingdoms." Another version says it this way, "You are my war club, my weapon for battle — with you I shatter nations, with you I destroy kingdoms." NIV

So, you see this journey was not easy — but necessary. God is still working on me, teaching me about His ways, and continually framing me to be who He has called me to be. "Thank you, Abba!"

Introduction to Why Flags

The root word "flag" means banner or standard and is interchangeable. It can also mean to gleam from afar, to raise a beacon, to be conspicuous, to flaunt, or to raise a flag. Flags have been used for centuries to mark territory or boundaries. It is also to signal the battlefield movements and to signal a message between ships.

Waving banners and worship flags are used in Christian and Davidic worship services (for more about Messianic Davidic Worship – refer to the section on dance). They form a type of holy wave offering to the Lord. Worshiping the Lord invites His presence; then we can come into agreement with what He is doing. It is the wave offering unto Him which shifts the atmosphere and releases breakthrough, healing, deliverance, joy, and the fire of God. Waving flags sets an atmosphere, depending on the color and movement of the flag. (There will be more information in the section about color.)

Flags are usually flown in pairs. It is a statement and declaration of agreement and unity. It increases awareness of the authority the Lord is giving us in the flag ministry.

Not only are the flags beautiful to look at, but their meaning is more important. Using flags in your personal time of prayer and worship is very important. It can include worship, intercession, and warfare.

What this book will help you do:

Why Flags

- To desire to worship God.
- To know that you are called to honor God through movement and dance.
- To have a heart for God.
- To realize that you are created and made to worship.
- To teach you what the flags mean and what the colors mean.
- To stir up the gift within you.
- To develop intimacy and closeness with the Father.
- To show you what the scriptures say about flags and banners.

So, relax, and kick your heels up! As you read this book, you will discover an abundance of scripture references given for each topic. There are sections included in the book to write notes for your convenience.

My prayer is that every reader allows the true teacher – the Holy Spirit – to help you understand and put movement to your expressions, develop intimacy and closeness with the Father, give you an understanding of praise and worship, and to stir up the gift within you.

Table of Contents

Let It Rain Flag..1

Glory And The Anointing Flag...2

Flame Flag (Red Flag)...3

Dance..4

The Expression of Flags...10

Spirit Of Breakthrough Flag..11

Praise..12

Angel Wings In Glory Flags...16

The Battle Cry..17

Fire Flags...18

Worship – Sound the Alarm!...19

Shekinah Glory Rods...22

How We Worship...24

God's Promises Flag..26

Spiritual Arsenal Army of Flags..27

Spiritual Missiles...28

Abundant Life Flag...29

Symbolic Colors of the Bible..30

Israeli Flag..34

Finger Ribbons..35

Flame Flags (Orange)..36

Joy Unspeakable Flags..37

Linda's Dance Tools...38

Afterword...40

About Linda..44

Let It Rain Flag

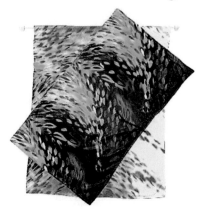

Refreshing From
The Throne Room of God

Deuteronomy 32:12
"Let my teaching drop as the rain,
my speech distill as the dew,
as raindrops on the tender herb,
and as showers on the grass."

Matthew 7:25
"and the rain descended, the floods came,
and the winds blew and beat on that house;
and it did not fall, for it was founded on the rock."

Ezekiel 34:26
"I will make them and the places all around My hill a blessing;
and I will cause showers to come down in their season;
there shall be showers of blessing."

Glory And The Anointing Flag

It is the sign of the Lord's blessing and prosperity.

Fresh oil from Heaven

The Anointing

Psalm 133:2
*"It is like the precious oil upon the head,
running down on the beard,
the beard of Aaron,
running down on the edge of his garments."*

Leviticus 8:12
*"And he poured some of the anointing oil on Aaron's head
and anointed him, to consecrate him.
And he poured of the anointing oil upon Aaron's head,
and anointed him, to sanctify him."*

The Glory

Psalm 19:1
*"The heavens declare the glory of God;
and the firmament shows His handiwork."*

Luke 2:14
*"Glory to God in the highest,
and on earth peace, goodwill toward men!"*

Flame Flag (Red Flag)

All Consuming Fire

Hebrews 12:29

"For our God is a consuming fire."

Luke 3:16

*"John answered, saying to all,
"I indeed baptize you with water;
but One mightier than I is coming,
whose sandal strap I am not worthy to loose.
He will baptize you with the Holy Spirit and fire."*

Dance

You must always remember that you are ministering before the Lord first. Dance is inspired by the Holy Spirit through music, prayer, and the Word of God; there is an expression of grace and power behind the expressive art form of dance (with fluid movement), and that can include the shout of exaltation to celebrate God's goodness and to encourage worship. Dance is an intimate, inward, and personal expression of love to the Father. It depicts a person passionately expressing their adoration for the Lord through dance.

The Benefits of Dance

- Deepens your spiritual walk – a one-on-one experience with the Lord.
- Enhances your private prayer time.
- Strengthens your expression of love and adoration to God.
- Brings refreshing joy and comfort.
- Promotes healing and restoration.

What Dance Is Not

It is not about worshiping the gift. Dancing should not be or become an idol. Although it is good to discover where your gifts and talents fit in the body of Christ – just because there is liberty and freedom to worship – be careful not to get caught chasing the gift and looking for an opportunity to demonstrate talent. Instead, wait and allow God to call for the creative arts. It is so essential to minister in spirit and in truth – not as an entertainer or performer.

Hebrew Words for Dance[2]

- KARAR – To dance or whirl. (2 Samuel 6:14)

- RAQAD – To stamp; spring about; dance; jump; skip. (1 Chronicles 15:29, Ecclesiastes 3:4)

- GIYL/GUWL – To spin round under the influence of joy. (1 Chronicles 16:31, Psalms 9:14)

- ALATS – To jump for joy; to be joyful; rejoice; to be triumphant. (Proverbs 28:12, Psalm 68:3)

---

[2] http://judahdancewear.com/5/Dance_in_the_Bible, 8/15/2019

Different Variations of Praise Dance

- **Joyous Victory Dance**
  Celebrates God's wonderful blessings! Often the congregation joins in jubilation.

  Psalm 95:6
  "Oh come, let us worship and bow down; let us kneel before the LORD our Maker."

- **Praise Dance**
  Expresses celebration to God, reverent and yielding.

  Psalm 35:18
  "I will give You thanks in the great assembly; I will praise You among many people."

- **Thankful Dance**
  Powerful and confident dance of strength – boldly declaring God's authority over the enemy with the flags and banners. It can ignite victorious breakthrough as with Israel's armies.

  Psalm 30:11
  "You have turned for me my mourning into dancing; you have put off my sackcloth and clothed me with gladness,"

- **Spontaneous Dance**
  Holy Spirit inspired dance, portraying a message from God.

  Psalm 149:3
  "Let them praise His name with the dance; let them sing praises to Him with the timbrel and harp."

- **Prophetic Dance**
  Significant with depth when done with purpose, and it takes on prophetic authority.

  1 Samuel 10:5-6
  "After that you shall come to the hill of God where the Philistine garrison *is*. And it will happen, when you have come there to the city, that you will meet a group of prophets coming down from the high place with a stringed instrument, a tambourine, a flute, and a harp before them; and they will be prophesying. ⁶ Then the Spirit of the LORD will come upon you, and you will prophesy with them and be turned into another man."

- **Warfare Dance**
  Invokes the presence of God and tears up the fallow ground, rends the Heavens, and causes signs and wonders and miracles to take place.

Chronicles 20:21

"And when he had consulted with the people, he appointed those who should sing to the LORD, and who should praise the beauty of holiness, as they went out before the army and were saying: "Praise the LORD, for His mercy *endures* forever."

Psalm 144:1

"Blessed be the Lord my Rock, who trains my hands for war, and my fingers for battle —"

- **Davidic Dance**

Illustrates joy and healing. We remember King David as he danced before the Lord in true freedom. Davidic worship dance is highly respected around the world.

2 Samuel 6:14-16

"Then David danced before the Lord with all *his* might; and David *was* wearing a linen ephod. [15] So David and all the house of Israel brought up the ark of the Lord with shouting and with the sound of the trumpet. [16] Now as the ark of the Lord came into the City of David, Michal, Saul's daughter, looked through a window and saw King David leaping and whirling before the Lord; and she despised him in her heart."

Notes

_____

_____

_____

_____

_____

_____

_____

_____

_____

_____

_____

_____

_____

The Expression of Flags

Minister To And Celebrate The Lord	Psalm 20:4-7; 1 Chronicles 16:4
The Lord Raises The Standard	Isaiah 59:19
Banners Bestow Honor	Psalm 60:4
A Proclamation	Jeremiah 50:2; 61:12
A Garment Of Praise	Isaiah 61:3
Signal Or Attract Attention	Jeremiah 4:6; 51:12
Declare Who You Represent	Numbers 1:52; 2:2; 10:14
Herald The Event	Isaiah 49:22
A Rallying Point Of Healing	Isaiah 11:10; John 3:14-15
Put The Enemy To Flight (Causes Fear Of The Lord)	Isaiah 31:8-9
Show Victories Won	Psalm 20:5-9
Rally The Troops In War	Isaiah 5:26; 11:12; 13:2; 30:17; 2 Chr. 20:20-22; Jeremiah 51:12, 27
Unify The Company – Directing The Warfare And Praise	Isaiah 13:2
Signal Of God's Presence	Exodus 17:5

- Jehovah-Nissi, You are my victory, my banner, and my standard (Exodus 17:15).
- Your banner over me is love (Song of Solomon 2:4).
- When the enemy shall come in like a flood, You will lift up a standard against him! (Isaiah 59:19)

Spirit Of Breakthrough Flag To Your Victory

God Provides A Way Out Of An Escape

2 Samuel 5:20

*"So David went to Baal Perazim,
and David defeated them there; and he said,
"The Lord has broken through my enemies before me,
like a breakthrough of water."
Therefore he called the name of that place Baal Perazim."*

Praise

Praise expresses adoration to give thanks. It allows you to enter into God's presence. Praise gets God's attention. It magnifies God and minimizes your problems. Praise shows God you are grateful. It brings silence to the enemy.

Seven Hebrew Words For Praise (Types of Praise):

- Halal (haw-lal) Most common word for **Praise**. This word means to praise, celebrate, sing praises or boast about. A group of people shouting in jubilation.

- Yadah (yaw-daw') To worship with **Thanksgiving** and with extended hands. It expresses thanksgiving because of God's acts of goodness.

- Tehillah (the-hil-law') It means **Adoration**, to praise by singing, act of general or public praises. It focuses on deeds or qualities that are worthy of praise and glory.

- Zamar (zaw-mar') It means to **Strike with Fingers,** touching the strings or touching other parts of musical instruments.

- Towdah (to-daw') It is an act of **Adoration** with extended hands, and it means confession, praise, thanksgiving through song or hymns.

Why Flags

- Shabach (shaw-bakh') It means to **Address in Loud Tone**; to praise, to commend or to congratulate means to **Triumph** through praise. Your praise prophesies your **Victory**.

- Barak (baw-rak') It means **Kneel**, a humble acknowledgment that God is the **Source** of all good things.

References: Psalm 150:6, Psalm 103:1, Hebrews 13:15, 1 Chronicles 16:9, Isaiah 55:12

Praise Honors God!	**Praise** Undergirds Faith!
Praise Brings Deliverance!	**Praise** Is the Voice of Faith!
Praise Is the Language of Heaven!	**Praise** Sets the Stage for God to Move!
Praise Releases the Angels to Minister!	**Praise** Fuels Joy, which is your Strength!
Praise Knocks down walls of resistance!	**Praise** Stills the enemy and the avenger!
Praise Dispels darkness and depression!	**Praise** Must precede, not follow blessings!
Praise Gives God the legal right to help you!	**Praise** Brings the presence of God onto the scene!
Praise Is a sure sign of acceptance of the Word of God!	**Praise** Is the highway that faith moves its blessings down!

Notes

Angel Wings In Glory Flags

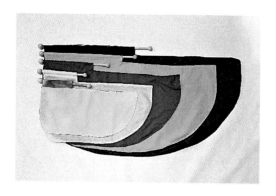

God's Protection

Psalm 91:4a
"He shall cover you with His feathers,
and under His wings you shall take refuge;"

Luke 4:10
"For it is written:
'He shall give His angels charge over you,
to keep you,'"

The Battle Cry

"Latent warrior, arise up and fight! Stand on the ground I have given you. This is the day you will see my works. This is the day you will step into the battlefield in My Name. You will speak the Word I give you, nothing added, and nothing taken away. I have made you, and I am releasing you for this time period. Prophecy is unfolding; time has been cut short. I release boldness, I release power, I release peace, I release joy, I release love, I release freedom. You are not bound by mistakes of the past. You are not bound by old paradigms. I have released new into your life. You are fresh, you are reborn, you are the NEW THING. You are what the world has been waiting for. I transformed your shyness into humility, I transformed your pride into prudence. Your confidence is based on Me, and your ability to rest in My Peace. I give unto you the garment of praise; I give unto you a song of victory. You are released into battle on a new front, a battle that you will see with your natural and spiritual eye. You shall see that which is hidden. You will break down what is covered in deceit. You will bask in My Glory, and ACT in My Glory. I am the LORD, and I have chosen you."

Prophetic Word given November 2011 through
Philip Thornton, Senior Pastor
Church Without Walls, now Legacy Faith Church
Harrisburg, Pennsylvania

Fire Flags

2 flags in 1

Having A Heart That Is On Fire For God.

Hebrews 12:28-29

*"Therefore, since we are receiving a kingdom
which cannot be shaken, let us have grace,
by which we may serve God acceptably
with reverence and godly fear.
29 For our God is a consuming fire."*

Psalm 97:3

*"A fire goes before Him,
and burns up His enemies round about."*

Worship – Sound the Alarm!

There is always a sound before there is a major move of God. Worship is the sound that goes forth in the atmosphere in our churches and in our personal time of prayer – the Battle Cry! That is where the enemy is defeated and where we receive victory over the enemy.

I would also like to mention the importance of personal study and personal worship. Just spending time in His presence, you loving Him and Him loving you establishes oneness with Him. In 1 Corinthians 6:17, it says, "But he who is joined [united] to the Lord is one spirit *with Him.*" In His presence is where your day-to-day victories are won.

Whenever we enter into God's presence, we must come with thanksgiving. Therefore, we must be careful not to be a bystander or spectator, because in worship (the holy place) God desires our participation. So it is imperative to step out, be bold in our approach to Him – exposing the enemy.

In an atmosphere of worship, there is a weightiness of God's presence that brings the manifestation of healing and restoration, peace, refreshing, and rest. In this place of intimacy and abandonment (surrender), there is happiness and joy, and ultimately there is nothing holding you back (but you).

Why Flags

The scriptures below are our guidelines:

- Psalm 103:1 – "Bless the Lord, O my soul; and all that is within me, bless His holy name!"

- John 4:23-24 – "But the hour is coming, and now is, when the true worshipers will worship the Father in spirit and truth; for the Father is seeking such to worship Him. [24] God is Spirit, and those who worship Him must worship in spirit and truth."

- Psalm 100:4 – "Enter into His gates with thanksgiving, and into His courts with praise. Be thankful to Him, and bless His name."

- Exodus 15:11 – "Who is like You, O Lord, among the gods? Who is like You, glorious in holiness, fearful in praises, doing wonders?"

- Psalm 99:5 – "Exalt the Lord our God, and worship at His footstool – He is holy."

- 1 Chronicles 16:29 – "Give to the Lord the glory due His name; bring an offering, and come before Him. Oh, worship the Lord in the beauty of holiness!"

Why Flags

"As I press into the place of Worship, my spirit man takes the lead to give God All the Honor that is due His name. My soul (will, mind, emotions) begins to immediately agree. Then my body responds. Worshiping Him is saying to God He is worthy and due All Glory that He has crowned me with. My faith by the Word of God enables me to press beyond any needs or wants and have a primary focus on Him alone. This Worship (for me) brings me into His presence, and in His presence is all I desire..."

David Payton, Jr., Senior Associate Pastor
Church Without Walls, now Legacy Faith Church
Harrisburg, Pennsylvania

Shekinah Glory Rods

*Shekinah means
Radiant Brilliant —
to magnify in worship.*

Revolving Rod For Transmitting

2 Corinthians 4:6

*"For it is the God who commanded light
to shine out of darkness,
who has shone in our hearts
to give the light of the knowledge of the glory of God
in the face of Jesus Christ."*

Haggai 2:9

*"'The glory of this latter temple shall be
greater than the former,' says the Lord of hosts.
'And in this place I will give peace,'
says the Lord of hosts."*

Notes

_____

_____

_____

_____

_____

_____

_____

_____

_____

_____

_____

_____

How We Worship

You may see people worshiping God in some unfamiliar ways. While some forms of worship may not be something that you will personally participate in, below is the scriptural basis for what you might experience. Please feel free to express your heart and worship in whatever way you are most comfortable.

- **Banners** – Psalm 60:4-5
- **Choir** – Ecclesiastes 2:8
- **Dancing** – Jeremiah 31:13
- **Instruments** – 1 Chronicles 13:8
- **Kneeling** – 1 Kings 8:54
- **Prostration** – 1 Chronicles 29:20
- **Quiet Stillness** – Isaiah 32:18
- **Raised Hands** – Psalm 141:2
- **Shout** – Psalm 98:4
- **Singing** – Psalm 28:7
- **Song of the Lord** – Zephaniah 3:17
- **Spontaneous Singing** – Psalm 149:1
- **Weeping** – Luke 7:28
- **Holy Laughter** – Proverbs 17:22a

Why Flags

"Worship is a feeling or expression of reverence and adoration for a deity and in my particular case lifting up my hands and voice in songs of praise to the Almighty God, El Shaddai, Creator of Heaven and Earth, Jesus Christ, My Redeemer, the Power of the Holy Spirit, the Sanctifier and Sustainer of my life. When I am in worship, it is a place of security where I am able to let my guard down and lay all that I am at the altar in total surrender to the Great I AM. In worship, I glorify and honor Elohim. When I am finished worshiping, I feel free – knowing that all is in God Almighty's hand. To worship God is an honor, privilege, and blessing. Worship brings me closer and closer to God and builds a more intimate relationship with God. He is an omnipresent God. For James 4:8 says if you draw nigh to him, then he will draw nigh to you. Jesus says that when I worship God, I must worship Him in spirit and in truth (John 4:24). I am a woman after God's heart and worshiping keeps me thirsty for more of His wonderful and everlasting love. It is in Worship that I am able to give my God Reverence, Honor, Adoration, and Praise. I pray to continue to Glorify God in Jesus Christ and in the Power of the Holy Spirit."

Gladys Ogwal

God's Promises Flag

A Release Of Promises In The Atmosphere

2 Peter 1:2-4

"Grace and peace be multiplied to you
in the knowledge of God and of Jesus our Lord,
³ as His divine power has given to us
all things that pertain to life and godliness,
through the knowledge of Him
who called us by glory and virtue,
⁴ by which have been given to us
exceedingly great and precious promises,
that through these you may be
partakers of the divine nature,
having escaped the corruption
that is in the world through lust."

Spiritual Arsenal Army of Flags

Arsenal Flag

Arsenal Shekinah Glory Rod

Tenesha
Arsenal Head Band

Sheila
Arsenal Head Band

Arsenal Flag
2 flags in 1

Arsenal Infinity Scarf

Spiritual Missiles

"People do not fully understand that their individual dance is a weapon and that they are breaking up ground and taking territory under the garment of praise. They do not fully understand the sound of the anointing in their voice is like a whiplash to the back of the enemy. They do not fully understand that as they wave their hands, they are waving the banner of the blood-stained victory. They have been taught to do these things, without the understanding and knowledge of what they mean. It is essential that we know there is power in knowledge.

Flags, dance, and worship are weapons in themselves. They lift up God and tear down the enemy's kingdom. When you give praise to God, it is like a spiritual missile that is hurled into the enemy's camp. It causes confusion and destruction. He hates and fights our praise.

Worship is a two-edged device! It sharpens your sword and breaks the edge off the enemy."

Prophetic Word given November 2011 through
Philip Thornton, Senior Pastor
Church Without Walls, now Legacy Faith Church
Harrisburg, Pennsylvania

Abundant Life Flag

I Have Come To
Give You Abundant Life

John 10:10

"The thief does not come except
to steal, and to kill, and to destroy.
I have come that they may have life,
and that they may have it more abundantly."

John 16:33

"These things I have spoken to you,
that in Me you may have peace.
In the world you will have tribulation;
but be of good cheer,
I have overcome the world."

Symbolic Colors of the Bible
Used in Worship

Color	Description	Scripture
Rainbow	God's Promises	Rev. 4:3
	Covenant	Gen. 9:13-14
Tabernacle	Old Dwelling	Ex. 26:1
	New Dwelling	1 Cor. 3:16
	New Jerusalem	Rev. 21:2-3
Blood Red	Jesus' Sacrifice	Acts 20:28
	Life Blood	Gen. 9:4
	Passover, Protection	Ex. 12:23
Wine or Deep Red	Sin	Isaiah 1:1
	Redemption	Gen. 38:28-29
	Pardon, Deliverance	Joshua 2:18
	Forgiveness	Heb. 9:22
Purple	Messiah's Royalty	John 19:2
	Kingship	Jud. 8:26
	Believer's Royalty	1 Pet. 2:9
	Priesthood	
Lavender	Standing in	Song of Sol. 4:14
	His Presence	
	Healing	
White	Purity, Righteousness	Dan. 12:10
(contains all colors)	Light, Festivity, Holy,	Dan. 7:9
	Salvation, Resurrection	Matt. 17:2
	Overcomer, Triumph,	Eccl. 9:8

Why Flags

	Bride's Garments	Zeph. 6:3
		John 20:12
		Rev. 3:5
		Rev. 7:9
		Rev. 19:8
Silver	Redemption	Matt. 27:3-9
Gold	Divine Nature	Rev. 3:18
Pearl	Treasure, Reward,	Matt. 13:44-46
	Gate, Doorway	Rev. 21:12
Clear, Transparent	Water Baptism	Matt. 3:11
	Wind, Holy Spirit	John 3:3, 5-7
	Born Again	
Orange Red (Flame)	Sacrifice of Prayer	Heb. 13:15
	Praise & Worship	1 Chr. 23:13
	Consuming Fire	Lev. 3:3
	Purify, Refine	Mal. 3:2
	Holy Spirit, Baptism	Acts 2:3
	Works Tested	1 Cor. 3:13
Pink/Light Red	Heart of Flesh	Eze. 11:19
Coral/Reddish	Red Sea, Exodus	Heb. 11:23
	Deliverance	Ex. 15:1,21
Yellow	God's Glory	Eze. 1:4, 8:2
		Ps. 68:13
Amber/Olive (Oil)	God's Anointing	Ex. 29:7
	Consecration	
Green	Life Everlasting	1 John 5:12
	Posterity	Ps. 37:35
	Flourish	Ps. 92:14

Why Flags

Royal Blue	God's Commandment	Num. 15:38
Sapphire Blue (Navy)	Divine Revelation	Ex. 24:10
Light Blue	Heaven, Heavenly	Eze. 1:26
Iridescent	Overcomer	Rev. 21:7, 27
	Rainbow/Promises	Rev. 4:3
	New Jerusalem	Rev. 21:11-19
	Precious Stones	
	Heavenly Treasure	
Brown/Wood	Humanity	Ex. 26:15
	Godly Offspring	Is. 11:1
		Jer. 23:5
Tan	Bread	Luke 22:19
	Communion	
	Yeshua (Jesus' Body)	
Brass/Copper	Tabernacle Altar	Ex. 38:30
	Atonement	Num. 21:9

This is a compilation of many interpretations of biblical color meanings. I pray that learning about the importance of these colors will release you into a deeper understanding of the impact that the colors bring.

Notes

_____

_____

_____

_____

_____

_____

_____

_____

_____

_____

_____

_____

Israeli Flag

The Shield Of David

Isaiah 11:10

*"And in that day there shall be a Root of Jesse,
who shall stand as a banner to the people;
for the Gentiles shall seek Him,
and His resting place shall be glorious."*

*What this verse is saying is . . . In the end times a
banner will be raised that will feature "the root of
Jesse" (the father of David). The flag will carry
the symbols of David and will act like a magnet
to draw the Jewish people back to their home. The
modern-day flag of Israel represents a fulfillment
of the Bible.*

Finger Ribbons

Praise The Lord Forever

Psalm 29:2
"Give unto the Lord the glory due to His name; worship the Lord in the beauty of holiness."

Psalm 150:6
"Let everything that has breath praise the Lord. Praise the Lord!"

Flame Flags *(Orange)*

2 flags in 1

Having An Ear That Is On Fire For God

Hebrews 12:28-29

*"Therefore, since we are receiving
a kingdom which cannot be shaken,
let us have grace, by which we may serve God
acceptably with reverence and godly fear.
²⁹ For our God is a consuming fire."*

Acts 2:3-4

*"Then there appeared to them divided tongues,
as of fire, and one sat upon each of them.
⁴ And they were all filled with the Holy Spirit
and began to speak with other tongues,
as the Spirit gave them utterance."*

Joy Unspeakable Flags

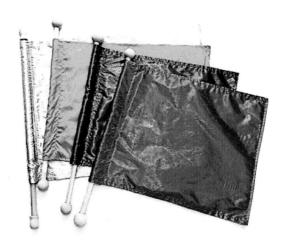

Praise Him

1 Thessalonians 5:16-18

"Rejoice always, [17] pray without ceasing,
[18] in everything give thanks;
for this is the will of God in Christ Jesus for you."

Psalm 118:24

"This is the day the Lord has made;
we will rejoice and be glad in it."

Linda's Dance Tools

Linda Donnelly
(717) 609-2623

Email: beholdhis@hotmail.com
Find us on Facebook:
Behold His Presence ~ custom
designed Dance, Worship Flags
and Banners ~

Examples of Linda's work:

Photos displayed from left to right

- Pendants
- Flags, Streamers and Glory Ribbons
- Shekinah Glory Rods
- Half Circle Angel Wing in Glory
- Finger Ribbons
- Fire Flag (2 flags in 1)

Ideal for Worshipers Ages 3-99
One-Stop Shop
Contact Linda for more finished products in her workshop.

Notes

_____

_____

_____

_____

_____

_____

_____

_____

_____

_____

_____

Afterword

Throughout scripture, God calls His people to raise a banner (standard, flag, ensign) in His name. He does this for several reasons:

<u>Flags Gather The People</u>:
"He will set up a banner for the nations, and will assemble the outcasts of Israel, and gather together the dispersed of Judah from the four corners of the earth." Isaiah 11:12

<u>Flags Are A Signal Or Form Of Communication</u>:
"Declare among the nations, proclaim, and set up a standard; proclaim – do not conceal it . . ." Jeremiah 50:2a

<u>Flags Are A Signal For Battle</u>:
"Set up a banner in the land, blow the trumpet among the nations! Prepare the nations against her [Babylon – the world's system], *call the kingdoms together against her: . . ."* Jeremiah 51:27a

<u>Flags Proclaim Victory</u>:
"We will rejoice in your salvation, and in the name of our God we will set up our banners!" Psalm 20:5a

Why Flags was written to explain the purpose of the flag ministry. In future writings, there will be in-depth teaching on how to minister using the flags.

Notes

_____

_____

_____

_____

_____

_____

_____

_____

_____

_____

_____

_____

Notes

_____

_____

_____

_____

_____

_____

_____

_____

_____

_____

_____

_____

Notes

About Linda

As Founder and Director of Behold His Presence, Linda has been ministering for the Lord through flags, banners, and dance since 2002. Her flag ministry experience has included conducting training classes and seminars for adults and children. Linda receives her inspiration and passion from the Holy Spirit.

Linda has received formal flag training from professional dance ministries and has instructed and orchestrated dance teams at national conferences, training centers, and churches.

Made in the USA
Middletown, DE
07 October 2024